Contnt

Fairfield Primary School, South Wigston

Bobby Lynam (6)	38
Vy Pham (6)	39
Oakley Palmer (6)	40
Ava Spencer (6)	41
Ray Basten (6)	42

Garston C of E Primary School, Garston

Finley Goldson (6)	43
Brooke Strode (6)	44
Niamh Mew (6)	45
Ohema Agyemang Addai-Tuffour (5)	46
Tsioh Atale (7)	47

Groombridge St Thomas' Church Of England Primary School, Groombridge

Oscar Turner (5)	48

Hewens Primary School, Hayes

Amritraj Ubha (6)	49

Highfields Primary School, Rowley Regis

Ibrahim Nauman (5)	50

Lucton School, Lucton

Benjy Powell (6)	51

Lyne & Longcross CE Primary School, Lyne

Grace Okoli (5)	52

Nelson Primary School, Ladywood

Ghassan Tabbara (7)	53
Halan Jamyani (6)	54
Sailusha Srinatha (5)	55
Adam Lakhdhar (7)	56
Abdul Kareem Koekoe (7)	57
Abbal Mahatra (6)	58
Ezhil Vendhan Manoj (5)	59
Almbrook Ibrahim (6)	60

New Monkland Primary School & Nursery, Glenmavis

Katie Hay (7)	61
Harper Fox (7)	62
Lee Porter (7)	63
Clara McLeod (7)	64
Christina Fagan (7)	65
Brody McCaffrey (7)	66
Lewis Gracey (6)	67

Orangefield Primary School, Belfast

Rudi Blackstock (7)	68
Elouise Bailie (7)	69
Jacob Wallace (6)	70
Charlie Sharpe (6)	71

Orleans Primary School, Twickenham

Shreyansh Satiale (7)	72

Outwoods Edge Primary School, Loughborough

Hafsa Moin (6)	73
Lois Smith (7)	74

Little Dreamers Acrostics

Poetic Stars

Edited By Debbie Killingworth

First published in Great Britain in 2025 by:

Young Writers
Remus House
Coltsfoot Drive
Peterborough
PE2 9BF
Telephone: 01733 890066
Website: www.youngwriters.co.uk

Foreword

Welcome Reader,

For Young Writers' latest competition Little Dreamers, we asked primary school pupils to write an acrostic poem. They could write about an animal, their favourite person, themselves or something from their imagination – anything at all! The acrostic is a fantastic introduction to poetry writing as it comes with a built-in structure, allowing children to focus on their creativity and vocabulary choice.

We live and breathe creativity here at Young Writers and we want to pass our love of the written word onto the next generation – what better way to do that than to celebrate their writing by publishing it in a book!

Featuring poems on a range of topics, this anthology is brimming with imagination and creativity, showcasing the blossoming writing skills of these young poets. They have brought their ideas to life using the power of words, resulting in some brilliant and fun acrostic poems!

Each awesome poet in this book should be super proud of themselves! We hope you will delight in these poems as much as we have.

Parkinson Lane Community Primary School, Halifax

Zunairah Ahtasham (5)	75
Muhammad Aziz (6)	76

Prospect Vale Primary School, Heald Green

Ada Kelly (5)	77

Ridgeway Primary School, Ridgeway

Jesse Gratton (5)	78
River Reynolds (5)	79
Jack Burke (5)	80

Seaton Academy, High Seaton

Imogen Ritchie (5)	81

Shoreditch Park Primary School, Hoxton

Myrto Parker (7)	82
Iasonas Parker (7)	83
Aras Doldur (6)	84

Spooner Row Primary School, Spooner Row

Teddy Weaver (5)	85
Eli Curtis George	86
Aaro Gage (5)	87
Jack Townsend (6)	88

St Anne's Catholic Primary School, Huyton

Joshua O'Neill (6)	89

St Anthony's Catholic Primary School, Kingshurst

Nancy Carroll (6)	90
Tommy Johnson (6)	91
Fabian Gloster (6)	92
Lewie Ward (6)	93

St Charles RC Primary School, Swinton

Freya O'Shea (5)	94
James Hampson (6)	95
Laura Wasielak (5)	96

St Francis Catholic Primary School, Shelfield

Elsa Humphries (6)	97
Albie Butler (6)	98
George Johnson (7)	99

St Michael's CE (A) Primary School, Tettenhall

Ewan Munro (6)	100
Logan Mancilla-Foulkes (6)	101

St Wilfrid's CE Primary School, Calverton

Ava Muligan (5)	102
Arthur Mooney (7)	103

Stockwell Primary School, Lambeth

Alma Abdillahi (6)	104
Itiel Arebalo Boutista (6)	105
Mayar Alsaleh (5)	106
Mario (7)	107
Alejandro Lopez Reyes (6)	108
Neziah Salmon Taylor (6)	109

Stuart Road Primary Academy, Stoke

Hunter Morgan (6)	110
Ezra Mayhew-Hiscock (6)	111

Tenterfields Primary Academy, Tenterfields

Charlotte Skipton (6)	112
Eva Dalbock (5)	113

The Coppice Primary School, Hollywood

Jonah Reid (6)	114

Whitechapel CE Primary School, Cleckheaton

Eva (6)	115

Worple Primary School, Isleworth

Elvis Gasulis-Faye (7)	116

The Poems

Cats

C urled up in a small fluffy ball
A ll snug and warm
T hinking of mice and milk
S lowly falling to sleep.

Abdul Qadir Shaikh (5)

Altmore Infant School, London

Teacher

T eachers teach the kids
E at the snack in maths
A nd the kids like the zzzs
C lasses like to play
H arry said, "When work is done
E at up, everyone."
R un, Harry.

Alex Melville (6)
Andrews Memorial Primary School, Comber

Scientist

S cience is the best!

C arefully making potions

I love science

E very type of science

N ever gets boring

T esting potions

I n the lab

S ometimes goes wrong

T he best job in the world.

Naomi Carty (6)
Berkswell C Of E Primary School, Berkswell

Nerf Gun

N ever want to stop playing
E veryone loves to play
R eally good time
F un

G reat
U nder
N erf guns away.

Harry Connors (6)
Berkswell C Of E Primary School, Berkswell

Kitten

K ind
I love kittens
T hey lick their paws
T ry to catch dogs
E at lots of fish
N apping all the time.

Milan Punian (6)

Berkswell C Of E Primary School, Berkswell

Chef

C ooking
H elping
E ating a bit
F lipping a frying pan.

Ethan Talagala (6)

Berkswell C Of E Primary School, Berkswell

Vet

V ery cute pets

E very pet is different

T iny ones and big ones.

George Robinson (7)

Berkswell C Of E Primary School, Berkswell

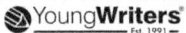
Cat

C ats are cuddly

A lways friendly

T iptoeing and walking are the hobbies of a cat.

Demi Olakanye (6)

Blessed Mother Teresa's Catholic Primary School, Highfields

Scientist

S cience is the best
C razy potions which are cool and amazing
I ndividual science which is very good
E xciting inventions which are amazing
N ew inventions and new experiments
T rying their best; some taste terrible
I ncredible thinking which is amazing
S uper cool and a tiny bit silly
T errific exploring which is cool.

Joya Dhillon (6)
Cherry Orchard Primary School, Birmingham

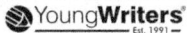

Basketballer

B lue Memphis jersey
A lliance
S lam dunk
K nockout king
E xcellent
T hree-point shooter
B ig and strong
A mbitious
L aMelo shoes
L ay-up shooter
E ven better at dunking
R ightfully rated.

Ajani Andrews (6)
Cherry Orchard Primary School, Birmingham

Tooth Fairy

T eeth
O n the pillow
O ver houses
T iny
H appy children

F lying
A t night
I see you sleeping
R eally small
Y ou need to sleep.

Alvina Islam (6)

Cherry Orchard Primary School, Birmingham

Footballer

F ield

O n the pitch

O ffside

T ouch the ball

B all

A ll together

L ook, I have the ball

L ots of people

E xercise

R eally fun.

Hamdan Waleed (6)

Cherry Orchard Primary School, Birmingham

Fisherman

F un

I ncredible

S uit

H elmet

E xploring new fish

R eady to do diving

M ore fish to catch

A t sea

N aughty fish can bite.

Adam Sharif (6)

Cherry Orchard Primary School, Birmingham

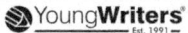

Vet

V ery careful with animals
E very animal is lovely
T ake care of the poor animals.

Hawaa Hussain (7)
Cherry Orchard Primary School, Birmingham

Nurse

N ice

U niform

R eally good

S miley

E veryone is happy.

Haya Sahak (6)

Cherry Orchard Primary School, Birmingham

Chef

C ooking skills
H at
E lite cook
F ood that is delicious.

Zayyan Sharif (6)
Cherry Orchard Primary School, Birmingham

Chef

C ooking skills
H at
E lite cook
F ood that is nice.

Khadijah Nur (6)

Cherry Orchard Primary School, Birmingham

Football

F ootball is my favourite sport

O ver the crossbar!

O wn goals

T he ball is rolling into the goal

B lasted into the back of the net

A way games

L eague table

L ove the game!

Storm Bond (6)

Cliffedale Primary School, Grantham

Dinosaurs

D inosaur Land

I t is scary

N ice dinosaurs

O range with red spotty dots

S ad dinosaurs

A lways eating

U nderground

R eally raining

S o spooky.

Skylar Mbanje (7)

Cliffedale Primary School, Grantham

Animals

A mazing animals
N ice vets help them
I love animals
M ammals are cute
A nimals make me happy
L emurs are my favourite
S quirrels climb up trees.

Amelia Weatherstone (5)
Cliffedale Primary School, Grantham

Monsters

M onster High is creepy

O ften spooky

N ever near humans

S care people

T ry to keep humans away

E pic adventure

R uin the city

S cary.

Millicent Nielsen (6)

Cliffedale Primary School, Grantham

Doctor

D octors are my mummy and daddy
O perations
C are
T ami loves doctors
O ften working in a hospital
R epair people when they are poorly.

Tami Tinuoye (5)

Cliffedale Primary School, Grantham

Football

F ootball

O n a pitch

O n

T he green grass

B alls

A re in the goal

L ike the game

L ike to play.

Bella Coleman (5)
Cliffedale Primary School, Grantham

Space

S pace is interesting
P lanets are everywhere
A liens live there
C olourful sky
E very star shines from space at night.

Charlotte Fahy (6)

Cliffedale Primary School, Grantham

Singer

S inger

I s singing

N eeds a microphone

G oes to a concert

E xcited to sing

R eally pretty blue dress.

Christina Tito (5)

Cliffedale Primary School, Grantham

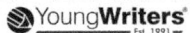

Space

S tars shining brightly
P lanets are big and colourful
A stronauts
C old and dark sky
E arth is big.

Rowan Fahy (6)
Cliffedale Primary School, Grantham

Enemy

E nemies are scary

N ot nice

E xtremely naughty

M ean

Y ou need to change!

Emmy Blaiklock-Morgan (7)

Cliffedale Primary School, Grantham

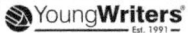
Space

S pace is cool
P lanets
A shooting star
C hasing the
E arth.

Meadow Bell (5)

Cliffedale Primary School, Grantham

Earth

E xciting

A lways spins

R eally big

T rees

H as humans.

Henry Marshall (6)

Cliffedale Primary School, Grantham

Footballer

F ootball is great.

O h yeah, football is awesome.

O livia that's my name, I love football.

T ennis, that's okay but football's better.

B est team in the world.

A wesome goal I scored.

L ove football, I love, love football.

L iverpool I'm playing against.

E very match is awesome.

R ight, let's go train.

Olivia Kelman (7)

Crombie Primary School, Westhill

Ghosts

G reat big ghosts and small ghosts.

H ow they scare some people.

O r some people like them.

S ome ghosts I am friends with.

T he ghost has a room to hide in.

S everal times I see him smile.

Isla George (7)

Crombie Primary School, Westhill

Harry

H elping everyone
A lways talking
R attling
R eading and writing
Y ummy.

Harry Budge (6)

Davenies School, Beaconsfield

Hairdress

H airdressing is what I want to do when I grow up

A nd make everyone's hair beautiful,

I have done someone's hair before,

R ed hair dye is beautiful

D oing hair is fun,

R unning to get the hair supplies

E very day, I do it,

S ometimes, I dye people's hair

S ometimes, I tie people's hair, each person's hair is different.

Evie Young (8)

Drumbowie Primary School, Falkirk

Dark

D ark rooms are scary
A bsolutely terrifying
R un as fast as you can
K eep away from dark rooms.

Finlay Young (10)

Drumbowie Primary School, Falkirk

Nerf

N erf guns are fun
E lectric Nerf guns are very cool
R apid fire bullets
F iring at my sister.

Aulay Anderson (9)

Drumbowie Primary School, Falkirk

My Toys

M y favourite toys are my Ninja Turtles
Y ay, a football

T he toy cars are fun
O fficer is good
Y es, my toy is cool
S ister is my best one.

Jayden Lim (7)

Eastern Primary School, Broughty Ferry

Dragon

D ragon

R oar loudly

A lways fly

G reen dragon

O range eyes

N oses that breathe fire.

Zoe Neave (7)

Eastern Primary School, Broughty Ferry

Morphing

M en screaming side to side
O thers cannot change
R ushing to freedom
P ower from their lair
H elping others, with no fear
I t makes me change places
N o one can find me
G runts the supervillain.

Bobby Lynam (6)
Fairfield Primary School, South Wigston

Footballer

F antastic players

O ffside

O ff the pitch

T ournaments

B all in the net

A mazing goalie

L eicester fox

L eicester stadium

E ngland are good

R unning players.

Vy Pham (6)

Fairfield Primary School, South Wigston

Football

F ootball rules

O ver the goal

O nside again

T eamwork

B all is kicked

A lways exciting

L ast minutes

L ove this game.

Oakley Palmer (6)

Fairfield Primary School, South Wigston

Witch

W ind blowing around

I nspiring broomstick

T oo scary

C at is her pet

H a, ha, ha, evil laugh.

Ava Spencer (6)

Fairfield Primary School, South Wigston

Fox

F erocious
O range fox
X ander is his name.

Ray Basten (6)
Fairfield Primary School, South Wigston

Gladiator

G ladiators is the best
L ooks nice
A mazing events
D rink water
I t is hard
A gainst contenders
T oday I play
O range juice
R unning after contenders.

Finley Goldson (6)

Garston C of E Primary School, Garston

Baker

B eautiful cooking.
A mazing chef.
K itchen to cook.
E pic cooking.
R ush cooking.

Brooke Strode (6)

Garston C of E Primary School, Garston

Singer

S ing

I t is amazing

N ice singer

G ood

E xciting

R eally fun.

Niamh Mew (6)

Garston C of E Primary School, Garston

Dream

D addy drinks.
R eegan red.
E xciting epic.
A rjun.
M ummy.

Ohema Agyemang Addai-Tuffour (5)
Garston C of E Primary School, Garston

Nurse

N urse

U nder

R uns

S cary

b **E** autiful.

Tsioh Atale (7)

Garston C of E Primary School, Garston

Pokémon

P ikachu Thunderbolt.

O cean Pokémon.

K ing of lightning.

É very Pokémon is different.

M y Pokémon cards are different.

O nly Pokémon cards are golden.

N o Pokémon is bad.

Oscar Turner (5)

Groombridge St Thomas' Church Of England Primary School, Groombridge

Palmer

P almer is my second favourite and Zola is first.

A nd have football skills.

L ove his skills.

M y passion is waiting for Chelsea to sign me up.

E nd of the FA Cup and it will be Chelsea's.

R unning to score a goal.

Amritraj Ubha (6)

Hewens Primary School, Hayes

Summer

S plashing in the water.

U nder blue skies.

M y friends are at the beach.

M elting ice cream.

E njoying a lot.

R eading a book and relaxing at the beach.

Ibrahim Nauman (5)

Highfields Primary School, Rowley Regis

Farmer

F armers do lots of hard work.

A nd they are important because they

R ide on tractors.

M unching up some wheat on the combine harvester.

E xtremely big tractors go farming.

R iding the tractors they go to fill their trailer up.

Benjy Powell (6)

Lucton School, Lucton

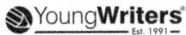
Teacher

T eachers are amazing
E verybody likes them
A lways listening
C aring and happy
H elping us to learn
E xciting and fun lessons
R eal-life heroes.

Grace Okoli (5)

Lyne & Longcross CE Primary School, Lyne

Science

S ometimes I wonder late at night,

C an we reach the stars, the planets and their sights?

I keep asking, is it possible, is it right?

E xploring the universe, and its shining light.

N ever will I stop gazing at the beautiful sight.

C urious I wonder, can we reach it and go beyond our height?

E ventually, I learned only science can answer and shed light!

Ghassan Tabbara (7)

Nelson Primary School, Ladywood

Art Teacher

A rt is peaceful.
R ainbow is a beautiful painting of the sky.
T he rainbow is colourful.

T hink that each colour shows variety.
E very colour has a song.
A rt is fun.
C olours speak of joy.
H umans are like rainbows.
E veryone loves a colour.
R ainbows tell us that we are beautiful together.

Halan Jamyani (6)
Nelson Primary School, Ladywood

Rainbow

R ainbows are incredible.

A ll are my favourite colours.

I wish I could slide down it.

N ature is more beautiful with rainbows.

B ig, perfect arch.

O nly a rainbow has seven colours.

W onderful light.

Sailusha Srinatha (5)

Nelson Primary School, Ladywood

Engineer

E ngineer, Adam, is brave.

N ever play with bricks.

G ood work Mr Adam!

I love my job.

N ew friends are here.

E at after work.

E njoy your lunch.

R aise your voice!

Adam Lakhdhar (7)

Nelson Primary School, Ladywood

Rainbow

R ed is my favourite colour.

A ny colour

I see will be exciting.

N ever be sad again.

B e very colourful.

O ver me there is a slide.

W hen you see a rainbow you say goodbye.

Abdul Kareem Koekoe (7)

Nelson Primary School, Ladywood

Friends

F riends make me always happy.
R eally nice and kind.
I nclude me in games.
E njoy playing with them.
N eed you.
D o things together.
S pecial and share.

Abbal Mahatra (6)

Nelson Primary School, Ladywood

Race Car

R eally fast.
A mazing.
C olourful.
E xciting to see.

C reate wonder.
A bsolute speed.
R apid.

Ezhil Vendhan Manoj (5)
Nelson Primary School, Ladywood

Doctor

D octors are helpful.

O utstanding.

C aring.

T he kindest.

O bedient.

R eally nice.

Almbrook Ibrahim (6)

Nelson Primary School, Ladywood

Unicorn

U nicorns are very fluffy

N ew baby unicorns, they are cute

I love baby unicorns and they are cute

C ute baby unicorns need to be loved

O nly the baby unicorns are asleep

R ainbow is awake and she is playing on a rainbow

N ow a baby unicorn is asleep.

Katie Hay (7)

New Monkland Primary School & Nursery, Glenmavis

Animals

A nimals go to the vet
N ew baby animals need a checkup
I want to be a vet
M y family doesn't have a vet
A nimals sometimes need to go to the vet
L oving animals makes me happy
S pecial animals need care.

Harper Fox (7)
New Monkland Primary School & Nursery, Glenmavis

Invisible

I want to be invisible

N o one can see me

V ery fun

I love my superpower

S o good

I want more powers

B ut my superpower is the best

L et's all play

E xcited all day.

Lee Porter (7)

New Monkland Primary School & Nursery, Glenmavis

Singer

S ome people take time to sing.
I 'm going to my concert.
N o pushing, the security guard might kick you out.
G o to a singer.
E lephants cannot sing.
R eturn to a singer.

Clara McLeod (7)

New Monkland Primary School & Nursery, Glenmavis

Spiders

S piders are hairy

P opping eyes on a spider

I saw a big spider

D o spiders scare you?

E ach spider is different

R eally scary spiders

S piders have eight legs.

Christina Fagan (7)

New Monkland Primary School & Nursery, Glenmavis

Heights

H eights are scary
E very little metre is scary
I don't like heights
G reat heights make me sick
H ave you got a fear?
T op of mountains
S ick of heights.

Brody McCaffrey (7)

New Monkland Primary School & Nursery,
Glenmavis

Nessie

N essie is very scary

E xtremely strong

S o ferocious

S o mean

I saw Nessie the other day

E xtremely good at hiding.

Lewis Gracey (6)

New Monkland Primary School & Nursery, Glenmavis

Family

F ootball with my dad on a Saturday.

A walk in the park with Mum and Dad and Raya

M y favourite place is Groomsport with everyone in my family

I love to play on the beach with my little cousin Jonah.

L ong days by the sea, Nanny, Granda and me.

Y our family is the most important thing in the world.

Rudi Blackstock (7)

Orangefield Primary School, Belfast

Dentist

D on't take me to the dentist
E louise doesn't like it
N eed to go every six months
T ime to go to the dentist
I don't want to go now
S orry, Mum
T he dentist will have to wait.

Elouise Bailie (7)

Orangefield Primary School, Belfast

Policeman

P olice help people
O bey the police
L ooking for bad guys
I like the police
C ool job
E mergency calls
M ake people feel safe
A rresting bad guys
N ee-naw!

Jacob Wallace (6)
Orangefield Primary School, Belfast

Shark

S wimming in water is what I do best

H unting down prey I do better than the rest

A fraid of me most humans are

R unning away if they see me near

K illing them all is what they fear.

Charlie Sharpe (6)

Orangefield Primary School, Belfast

Lioness

L ast night, I had a funny dream
I saw a lioness nearby, a scream
O h my God, she had an ice cream
'N' I asked her, "Will you give me some?"
"E ww," said she 'n' kicked my bum
S o I ran home 'n' told my mum
S he laughed 'n' said it was a dream.

Shreyansh Satiale (7)

Orleans Primary School, Twickenham

Friends

F ind your own helpful friends.

R ide bikes together.

I t's kind to help friends.

E at with your friends.

N ever say bad words to your friends.

D on't end friendships!

S ay kind and nice words to friends.

Hafsa Moin (6)

Outwoods Edge Primary School, Loughborough

Wasps

W asps are mean.

A re strong.

S ting.

P ersonal.

S pace.

Lois Smith (7)

Outwoods Edge Primary School, Loughborough

Teacher

T houghtful thinker
E xcellent at teaching
A wesome children
C aring to everyone
H elping kids to learn
E qual opportunities
R espected by all.

Zunairah Ahtasham (5)
Parkinson Lane Community Primary School, Halifax

Police

P rotect people day and night
O n the streets in dark and light
L oyal to their duty
I n hard times
C ourage they show
E nsuring everyone's safety.

Muhammad Aziz (6)

Parkinson Lane Community Primary School, Halifax

Trick

T rick or treat

R ain falls down

I like Halloween

C old and chilly

K ind of cosy.

Ada Kelly (5)

Prospect Vale Primary School, Heald Green

Museum

M ummy takes me.

U nderstand new things.

S ometimes Daddy takes me.

E yes have so much to see.

U ses lots of machines.

M akes me happy.

Jesse Gratton (5)

Ridgeway Primary School, Ridgeway

Cats

C an bite.

A lways jumping.

T eeth are sharp.

S cratch with claws.

River Reynolds (5)

Ridgeway Primary School, Ridgeway

Cars

C ars are fun.

A mazing.

R eally fast.

S hiny and colourful.

Jack Burke (5)

Ridgeway Primary School, Ridgeway

Space

S tars are shining

P lanets are moving

A stronauts can go to space

C omets are fast

E arth is our home.

Imogen Ritchie (5)

Seaton Academy, High Seaton

Fire Of London

F ierce fires growing everywhere
I n the city of London
R unning away for safety
E veryone in big London

O nly the ones fighting remain
F ire of fear comes to conquer London

L ondon will be miserable torture if no hero comes
O nly the bravest people will survive
N o one will be staying in their homes
D iaries tell us the lazy mayor lay in bed
O nly the maid and sixpence died
N o one was as grateful to see the fire gone.

Myrto Parker (7)

Shoreditch Park Primary School, Hoxton

Fire Of London

F ire spreading everywhere
I n the city of London
R aging flames uncontrollable
E veryone fled their homes

O nly somewhat dreaming
F ire on the dusty floor

L ondon cannot survive
O nly the River Thames can survive
N o one gets to their home safe
D iaries of Samuel Pepys tell us what
happened
O n the broken floor
N o one has forgotten.

Iasonas Parker (7)
Shoreditch Park Primary School, Hoxton

Fire Of London

F ire spreading quickly
I n a bakery the fire started
R aging flames began in it
E veryone fled their homes

O nly Samuel Pepys wrote
F irefighter

L ondon was old
O ld London fell down
N ever forgot the Great Fire of London
D id people escape?
O n the streets of London people died
N ew London.

Aras Doldur (6)

Shoreditch Park Primary School, Hoxton

Dinosaurs

D inosaurs

I n the night.

N o going near dinosaurs.

O n land.

S ploshing

A nd stomping.

U p high in the sky.

R unning fast.

S tomping.

Teddy Weaver (5)

Spooner Row Primary School, Spooner Row

Running

R acing on the track
U nder the sun
N ike shoes
N ear the end
I want to win
N o stopping
G old medal!

Eli Curtis George
Spooner Row Primary School, Spooner Row

Racing

R acing car.

A ston Martin.

C ool colours.

I nteresting tracks.

N o fear.

G o, go, go!

Aaro Gage (5)

Spooner Row Primary School, Spooner Row

Lego

L et's build together
E veryone's having fun
G eometric blocks everywhere
O h my goodness, such fun!

Jack Townsend (6)

Spooner Row Primary School, Spooner Row

Football

F antastic and fun.

O n the pitch.

O h I love it!

T errific tackles.

B ouncing ball.

A nother goal.

L oud noises.

L ove Liverpool.

Joshua O'Neill (6)

St Anne's Catholic Primary School, Huyton

Disneyland

D elightful food.

I t is fun.

S weets are sour.

N ew memories.

E lsa the ice queen.

Y ou will never forget.

L and of fun.

A place of magic.

N everland.

D opey from the Seven Dwarfs.

Nancy Carroll (6)

St Anthony's Catholic Primary School, Kingshurst

Football

F lying

O ut-of-this-world skills.

O ver the line.

T iming has to be right.

B irmingham City!

A lways supporting my team.

L aughing with my friends.

L et's cheer.

Tommy Johnson (6)

St Anthony's Catholic Primary School, Kingshurst

Football

F oot power
O ver the line
O pen your eyes
T ackle and slide
B ouncing around the pitch
A ttack the ball
L ots of cheering fans
L et's celebrate.

Fabian Gloster (6)

St Anthony's Catholic Primary School, Kingshurst

Candy

C hocolate-covered lollipops

A rms full of sweet treats

N ice, fluffy cotton candy

D on't eat too much

Y ummy, scrummy sugar dummy.

Lewie Ward (6)

St Anthony's Catholic Primary School, Kingshurst

Astronaut

A s good as the moon
S trawberries
T V screen
R ocket in space
O range and green aliens
N ight sky
A nimals in my ship
U mmm
T igers on my planet.

Freya O'Shea (5)

St Charles RC Primary School, Swinton

Tram Driver

T esting
R unning late
A hat
M an on the tram

D reaming
R inging the bell
I n the cabin
V ery happy
E very day
R ight on time.

James Hampson (6)
St Charles RC Primary School, Swinton

Mummy

M aking cakes
U nwell children
M arvellous
M emories
Y our friends will come.

Laura Wasielak (5)

St Charles RC Primary School, Swinton

Unique

U nderstanding when I know what you mean
N ice to people who are hurt
I nterested when I am writing
Q uick when I have lots of energy
U npredictable sometimes at school
E njoys family hugs every day.

Elsa Humphries (6)
St Francis Catholic Primary School, Shelfield

Unique

U nderstanding
N eat
I nterested
Q uick at running
U npredictable
E njoys going to Walsall matches.

Albie Butler (6)

St Francis Catholic Primary School, Shelfield

Unique

U nderstanding

N eat

I nterested in football

Q uestioning

U npredictable

E nergetic.

George Johnson (7)

St Francis Catholic Primary School, Shelfield

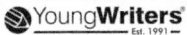

Scientist

S pecial
C lever
I nteresting
E xciting experiments
N ew ideas
T ries new things
I love it
S mart
T ime to explore.

Ewan Munro (6)

St Michael's CE (A) Primary School, Tettenhall

Monster

M essy

O nline

N ot nice

S cary and creepy

T hey are horrible

E vil

R ed spikes on its hand.

Logan Mancilla-Foulkes (6)

St Michael's CE (A) Primary School, Tettenhall

Marshmallow

M arshmallows are squidgy

A nd are fluffy too!

R eally tasty and chewy.

S weet

H ave them on top of a hot chocolate

M y mummy likes them

A nd eating them makes me happy

L ike a cloud

L oved by all

O n top of a biscuit to make a s'more

W ow, that's the tastiest treat of all!

Ava Muligan (5)

St Wilfrid's CE Primary School, Calverton

Yummy Food

Y ellow bananas

U gh, onions are disgusting

M arvellous mangoes

M elons are yummy

Y um, yum, yum

F abulous pizza

O ranges are juicy

O ctopus is tasty

D elicious, juicy apples.

Arthur Mooney (7)

St Wilfrid's CE Primary School, Calverton

Misbehaviour

M y day is going bad
I am in trouble
S o now I am sad
B ut I will try to be good!
E veryone saw and understood
H opefully, I get better
A nd get some sweets from my mother
V ery good, you can be too
I n the future, I will always be good
O n Tuesday, I was good
U ncle was happy
R est in my heart.

Alma Abdillahi (6)

Stockwell Primary School, Lambeth

Candyland

C andyland is made of candy
A nimals live in Candyland
N othing else lives in Candyland
D inner is the only thing they eat
Y es, the animals wanted to eat
L ater, they arrested a pig
A nd then the pig felt sad
N o one else went to jail
D efinitely felt sad and worried.

Itiel Arebalo Boutista (6)
Stockwell Primary School, Lambeth

Doctor

D ressed like an angel

O ld people might be sick

C ompassion and humanity

T ogether, they know what medication is right

O vercome health problems

R espect their patients.

Mayar Alsaleh (5)

Stockwell Primary School, Lambeth

Artist

A mazing work
R ealistic
T rying their best
I llusion
S uper good art
T ry really, really hard to do their best.

Mario (7)
Stockwell Primary School, Lambeth

Superhero

S uper
U nder
P ut
E xciting
R eal
H ard
E scape
R ead
O range.

Alejandro Lopez Reyes (6)
Stockwell Primary School, Lambeth

Lions

L ike them so much
I ntense and strong
O pinions are smart
N ice and clean
S ize is big.

Neziah Salmon Taylor (6)

Stockwell Primary School, Lambeth

Fairies

F lying in the sky
A cts and sings
I like them
R eally tiny
I ncredible clothes
E xciting and magic
S pecial wings.

Hunter Morgan (6)

Stuart Road Primary Academy, Stoke

Fish

F ood.

I like fish.

S mall.

H ome in the sea.

Ezra Mayhew-Hiscock (6)

Stuart Road Primary Academy, Stoke

Seaside

S unshine

E njoying

A nother lovely day

S unny and bright

I ncredible

D ay out

E xtra amazing.

Charlotte Skipton (6)

Tenterfields Primary Academy, Tenterfields

Dolls

D olls
O ld
L ittle
L ovely
S weet.

Eva Dalbock (5)

Tenterfields Primary Academy, Tenterfields

Football

F ootball is fun.

O nly score goals.

O ften do a celebration.

T ake one or two touches only.

B eautiful goals and beautiful pass.

A lways pass and shoot and tackle.

L ook at the ball.

L ove your team.

Jonah Reid (6)

The Coppice Primary School, Hollywood

Horses

H orses are brown.

O ften have a long tail.

R eally good runners.

S uper good jumpers.

E very horse eats hay.

Eva (6)
Whitechapel CE Primary School, Cleckheaton

Explorer

E nough.

e **X** traordinary me.

P laying.

L oving.

O ne.

R esilience.

E legant.

R uns.

Elvis Gasulis-Faye (7)

Worple Primary School, Isleworth

Young Writers Information

We hope you have enjoyed reading this book – and that you will continue to in the coming years.

If you're the parent or family member of an enthusiastic poet or story writer, do visit our website **www.youngwriters.co.uk/subscribe** and sign up to receive news, competitions, writing challenges and tips, activities and much, much more! There's lots to keep budding writers motivated!

If you would like to order further copies of this book, or any of our other titles, then please give us a call or order via your online account.

Young Writers
Remus House
Coltsfoot Drive
Peterborough
PE2 9BF
(01733) 890066
info@youngwriters.co.uk

Join in the conversation!
Tips, news, giveaways and much more!

f YoungWritersUK   **X** YoungWritersCW   **◉** youngwriterscw

♪ youngwriterscw   **▶** youngwriterscw-uk